Cornerstones of Freedom

The Story of
THE
GOLDEN SPIKE

By R. Conrad Stein

Illustrated by Tom Dunnington

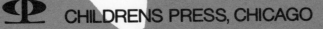

CHILDRENS PRESS, CHICAGO

Library of Congress Cataloging in Publication Data

Stein, R   Conrad.
  The story of the golden spike.

  (Cornerstones of freedom)
  SUMMARY: Relates the events surrounding the completion
of the world's first transcontinental railroad at
Promontory, Utah, in 1869.
  1. Union Pacific Railraod—Juvenile literature.
2. Central Pacific Railroad—Juvenile literature.
[1. Railroads—History] I. Dunnington, Tom.
II. Title.
HE2791.U55S73   385'.0973   78-4042
  ISBN 0-516-04621-7

Two train engines stood facing each other, headlight to headlight, on a single track on the morning of May 10, 1869. They had met on a dusty plain in the Far West. A crowd had gathered and a military band was ready to play. Millions of spikes had been driven into thousands of ties to build this first railroad connecting the Atlantic and the Pacific oceans. The last spike, to be driven this day, would be a gold one.

Telegraph operators waited to click off the news that the great Pacific Railroad was finally completed. The event would touch off parades and celebrations all over the country. In San Francisco writer Bret Harte was moved to compose a poem that began with these words:

What was it the engines said,
Pilots touching, head to head,
Facing on the single track,
Half a world behind each back?

The first transcontinental railroad was the greatest engineering feat yet accomplished by the young American republic. It opened the vast frontier to settlement. It also made fortunes for a few greedy railroad owners and many corrupt politicians.

Fifteen years earlier, railroad tracks had pushed up from the Atlantic Coast to the Mississippi River. Just a few years before that, a dreamer named John Plume had asked the United States Congress to authorize the building of a transcontinental railroad. Railroading in America was young then, and most Congressmen

laughed at the suggestion. One said it would be "like building a railroad to the moon."

Attitudes changed, however, when railroad tracks stretched as far as the Mississippi. The Union Pacific Railroad Company certainly was confident, and immediately started building a bridge across the river at the town of Rock Island, Illinois. Here the railroad faced a serious challenge. Since the opening of the Erie Canal, ships had been the prime movers of American goods. Steamship owners had become wealthy and powerful, particularly on the Mississippi. They would not stand idly by and watch their business go to the upstart railroads.

It took nine months to build the fifteen-hundred-foot bridge at Rock Island. When it was finished, railroad men cheered and steamship owners sulked.

The bridge had been completed for only two weeks when the steamboat *Effie Afton* crashed into one of its upright supports. The steamboat's furnace toppled over and within minutes the wooden bridge caught fire. Townspeople were fascinated as flames roared and the main span of the bridge crashed into the river.

As the bridge burned, steamship captains cruising nearby blew their whistles in triumph. One of them displayed a carefully lettered banner reading: MISSISSIPPI BRIDGE DESTROYED. LET US ALL REJOICE. The next day, the owner of the steamboat that had been destroyed during this "accident" went to court charging that the

bridge supports created currents that made passage of steamships dangerous.

The Union Pacific needed a good lawyer. Thomas Durant, one of the owners, went to Springfield, Illinois, and gave the case to an ambitious attorney named Abraham Lincoln.

Lincoln visited Rock Island and stood at water level watching the river flow under the charred bridge. A curious teenaged boy asked him what he was doing, and Lincoln immediately employed him. He had the boy throw brush and logs into the river upstream. He himself watched the debris pass under the bridge. Lincoln observed no unusual currents, and became convinced that the *Effie Afton* had been deliberately crashed into the bridge by a jealous steamship owner.

In court, Lincoln argued that the railroads had as much right to build bridges spanning rivers as steamships had to travel up and down them. The future President, a master in the courtroom, won his case. Power now passed to the railroad industry, and the once-mighty steamship owners would forever take a back seat.

When Lincoln became President a few years later, he remained a friend to the railroads.

Powerful members of Congress bought stock in railroad companies. Still others bought up cheap land in the West, speculating that the value of the land would skyrocket when railroads ran through it.

Railroad fever swept the country. No one doubted now that a transcontinental railroad would soon be in operation.

Work on the railroads skidded to a halt when the United States exploded in a bitter Civil War. For the next four years, the country was caught up in a whirlwind of violence as one bloody battle followed another.

Even as the war raged, however, a new railroad company was being formed in the West. Leland Stanford, who would later become governor of California, headed a group of Sacramento businessmen who established the Central Pacific Railroad Company. With one company in the West, and another in the East, the stage was set for a rivalry that would thrill the nation.

Bells tolled when the Civil War ended, but Thomas Durant was not listening. He needed an overseer, a construction boss who would be able to supervise the building of the Union Pacific

Railroad. Thousands of newly discharged soldiers were eager to work. They were strong men, made fierce by the harsh Civil War. Only a tough boss would be able to handle them.

Durant found not one, but two such men. Jack Casement was only five feet, four inches tall. His brother Dan was even shorter. But both were iron-willed fist fighters. Jack Casement had been a railroad construction worker before the war. During the war he had risen through the ranks to become a general. The two Casement brothers would be able to handle the toughest gang of workers.

In the West, the Central Pacific had an overseer named Charlie Crocker. He was a short-tempered man, built like a bull.

The Central Pacific, unlike the Union Pacific, had a problem finding workers. California was under-populated during the 1860s. Many of the men in the state were gold seekers or drifters who were unwilling to work long hours for the low pay offered by the railroads.

One day an associate of Crocker's suggested that he hire some of the Chinese laborers who lived in run-down sections of San Francisco.

"The Chinese are too small." Crocker replied. "They eat only rice. They're not strong enough."

"A long time ago the Chinese were strong enough to build a huge wall in China," said the other man.

Crocker, no student of history, replied, "Oh yeah? Tell me more about this wall."

A group of fifty Chinese were hired so Crocker could find out if they were strong enough to do the work. Crocker checked their progress after three grueling twelve-hour days. He quickly hired fifty more.

American workers became insulted. They threw down their shovels and hammers at the sight of the smiling Chinese laborers. Crocker gladly replaced them with more Chinese. Soon nine of every ten workers on the Central Pacific Railroad were Chinese. As the demand for labor grew, practically every Chinese male in the state of California was given a railroad job, and it was rumored that the Central Pacific had sent two ships to China to bring back more workers.

Crocker was pleased. The Chinese worked hard and did not strike. They also seemed to be genuinely happy working for two dollars a day.

Years later, after the golden spike had finally been driven, the gruff Crocker admitted that he had grown fond of the gentle Chinese.

In the spring of 1866, ships brought rails, train engines, and tools to the port of San Francisco. In the East, factories that had been producing cannon started churning out miles and miles of rails. The war was over and railroad fever struck again. The Central Pacific in the West and the Union Pacific in the East were poised like two runners in starting blocks. The race was on.

Each of the giant companies rushed to construct more miles of track than the other. No doubt pride was a factor in their competition, but money was an even more important factor. In 1862 Congress passed the Pacific Railway Act. Under the act, the companies would receive "subsidies" of from $16,000 to $48,000, depending on the terrain, for every mile of track they completed. They were also given huge sections of land absolutely free. Many Congressmen who were stockholders in the railroads would make fortunes.

Workers flocked to the Union Pacific for jobs. Many had been born in Germany or Poland. Still others were newly freed slaves. But the overwhelming majority were Irish. Before the Civil War, thousands of Irish had immigrated to the United States. Many of them worked on the railroads in the East. They had put down their tools to fight in the war, but now they returned to build the greatest railroad ever.

The Irish liked to work. They also liked to drink, gamble, and dance. The railroads ushered in the most colorful era in United States history—the days of the Wild West.

The town of North Platte, Nebraska did not exist until winter halted the construction of the Union Pacific in 1866. Then, almost overnight, more than one hundred wooden buildings were hammered together and lined up into streets. Dance halls, gambling places, saloons, and hotels sprang up as if they had been hiding under the ground. The Union Pacific crew numbered about two thousand men, and many slick operators wanted a share of their wages.

Every night fights broke out over the gambling tables. A visiting Englishman noted, "The greatest amusement here (North Platte) seems to be the practice of shooting one another."

Other towns appeared out of nowhere. Some were built even before the railroad tracks arrived. The gamblers and saloon owners knew the route the railroads would take, so they set up shop and waited for the tracks to catch up. Some of these towns would last for no more than a few weeks. Others will live forever in western lore —Abilene, Cheyenne, Laramie, Medicine Bend.

The names that became cowboy legends followed the railroads westward. Because the Union Pacific needed meat to feed its husky Irish workers, a young man was hired to hunt buffalo. He was a crack shot named William Cody. Cody became such an efficient buffalo killer that he earned the nickname "Buffalo Bill." Abilene, Kansas was both a railhead and a cattle town. It marked the end of the long trail drives where cowboys were paid. Several shootings a night were common in the heyday of Abilene. Finally the citizens elected a new mayor, James Butler "Wild Bill" Hickok. Not even the most drunken cowboy or railroad worker would tangle with Wild Bill, and peace came to the most lawless town in the West.

Mile by mile, the Union Pacific pushed over the prairies, a single track heading west. To carry supplies, the Casement brothers invented the "work train." Ten to fifteen cars were attached to an engine. Some were flat cars loaded with rails. Another was a "chuck wagon" car where food was prepared. Still another was outfitted as a blacksmith's shop. This special train followed the workers and chugged foward as soon as new track was hammered down.

Soon the Union Pacific crew was laying more than a mile of track a day. Not satisfied, the Casement brothers offered their men bonuses. Instead of the usual two dollars, they would receive three dollars a day if they could lay a mile and half of track, and four dollars a day if they could manage two.

On the other side of the country, Charlie Crocker fumed. His Chinese workers were bogged down digging a long tunnel through the Sierra Mountains. At the rate they were going, the Union Pacific would be in California before the Central Pacific got beyond the Sierras.

During the winter of 1867, the Central Pacific made an important move. They kept one crew chipping away at the tunnel while they sent Crocker and three thousand Chinese laborers over the Sierra Mountains, on foot or on horseback, to start laying track on the other side. This meant that all their equipment—rails, spikes, hammers, and food—would have to be carried with them over the snowy peaks.

The most incredible single accomplishment during the building of the transcontinental railroad was the transporting of three train engines and forty railroad cars over the snow-covered Sierras. They were carried by the Central Pacific's Chinese laborers. The trains and cars were dismantled as much as possible and lashed onto sleighs. Horses, mules, and men inched the sleighs up to the top of the mountain and lowered them down again. When sleighs that were large enough could not be found, logs were used to carry the load. Somehow, Crocker and his men managed to move enough equipment over the mountain that winter to lay fifty miles of track the following spring.

In the East, the Union Pacific rolled steadily westward until it ran into Indian country. While Congress was giving away generous amounts of land to the railroads, they ignored the fact that they had given the same land to the Indians only a few years earlier.

More than the cattlemen and more than the farmers, the Indians hated the railroads. They guessed, rightly, that the puffing and steaming Iron Horses signaled the end of their way of life. For decades they had been pushed farther and farther west. Now the white men were nailing iron rails into land that had been promised to them. This time the Indians had nowhere else to go.

Bloody shoot-outs flared up between Indians and railroad crews. During one attack, a band of Indians chased a dozen railroad workers inside a wooden shed that housed a train engine. The Indians set fire to the shed, hoping to drive the workers out. Instead, the men climbed aboard the engine. The engineer got up steam, crashed his Iron Horse through the closed door of the shed, and sped down the track.

Help came to the railroads from the United States Cavalry. General Philip Sheridan, who hated Indians, sent patrols roving about railroad construction sites with orders to shoot Indians on sight. Rarely did the cavalry distinguish between peaceful Indians and rampaging ones. In November of 1868, an ambitious colonel named George Custer destroyed a Cheyenne village, even though the Indians put up almost no resistance.

In the Far West, the Central Pacific had no problems with the Indians. When curious Indians came near the work camps, Charlie Crocker hired them. It was not that Mr. Crocker believed in fair employment practices; he simply needed every hand he could get.

Though European Americans refused to work with the Chinese, native American worked with them easily. Only one problem occurred. Late one night, when the men were exchanging stories over the campfire, one Indian told a Chinese worker that in the Nevada desert there were snakes so large they could swallow a man in one gulp. The next morning Charlie Crocker discovered that his crew was short about five hundred Chinese. Someone told him what had happened the night before. He saddled his horse and rode out to intercept the Chinese, who were following the rails back to California. As he galloped out of camp he shouted a curse at the Indians and their love of telling tall tales.

In the summer of 1868 the great race heated up. The Central Pacific slammed down tracks in Nevada while the Union Pacific hammered away in Wyoming. The goal of each company was to reach the state line of Utah.

Telegraph lines followed the railroads, and newspaper reporters from the East camped with the construction crews. Readers in eastern cities, who had grown accustomed to following maps marking battle lines during the Civil War, now read about each exciting mile of track being laid down by the two rival companies. Practically everyone in the country had a bet on which company would reach Utah first.

Down the stretch came the great race. It pitted East against West, and Irish against Chinese. It was said that the Union Pacific ran on whiskey, and the Central Pacific ran on tea.

As the race became more intense, the two companies became more wasteful. A properly built railroad digs "cuts" through hills to keep the track straight. But cuts take time to dig, so the Central Pacific laid their track around the hills. "So what?" said a company engineer. "The government's paying by the mile." The Central Pacific's track soon resembled a giant snake, and millions of dollars would later be spent to straighten out the rails.

Winter came early in 1868 and the Union Pacific found the ground covered with snow and ice. That did not stop the track layers, who hammered their ties and rails directly into the ice. When spring came, whole sections of track were dangling in the air. Lives were lost as tracks gave way and trains tumbled down mountains.

As the competition grew fiercer, the Union Pacific hoped that the injection of racism would get more work out of their exhausted crews. When fatigue slowed down their men one of the Casement brothers would shout, "You gonna let a bunch of little Chinamen beat you to Utah?"

"No!" came the hearty reply, and tired muscles strained again.

The Union Pacific crossed the state line of Utah first, but by then a second race was in the making. This race involved Thomas Durant, one of the owners of the Union Pacific, and Charlie Crocker, construction boss of the Central Pacific. Durant liked to gamble and Crocker liked to brag. One day Crocker claimed that his men could lay ten miles of track in one day.

Impossible, thought Durant. Two years earlier crews were averaging one, perhaps two, miles a day. Now that the men had had years of experience they could lay down five or even six miles in one twelve-hour shift. But ten miles in one day? No crew could accomplish that.

Durant bet Crocker ten thousand dollars that his Central Pacific laborers could not lay ten miles of track in one day.

It was cool on the morning of April 28, 1869. At seven o'clock that morning the men of the Central Pacific started slamming down track over the flat plains of Utah. At one-thirty Crocker halted work for lunch. The crew had already completed six miles. By seven that evening, the Central Pacific had laid down ten miles of track plus some fifty odd feet. It was a record that no railroad construction crew would ever beat. Someone with a head for figures noted that in one day 25,800 ties had been laid down, 3,520 rails had been spiked to them, and that each rail handler had lifted 250,000 pounds. No one even tried to count the number of spikes driven.

Durant, a millionaire, paid Crocker ten thousand dollars. Crocker shook the hand of every laborer on the Central Pacific.

After much bickering, the two railroad companies finally agreed on a meeting place. They chose a dusty, isolated spot in the Promontory mountain range of Utah. For the occasion the spot was called Promontory Point. Here the golden spike would be driven and the great race would end. Golden spikes marked the completion of many other important railroads. They never remained in the tracks. They were quickly removed and replaced by steel spikes. Golden spikes are now displayed in railroad museums throughout the country.

Champagne flowed freely on the morning of May 10, 1869. A huge crowd gathered. There were hundreds of swaggering Irishmen and hun-

dreds of Chinese clad in their blue work uniforms and cone-shaped hats. Four companies of infantry and a brass band stood at attention. About thirty well-dressed railroad dignitaries and their wives milled about the spot where the final spike would be driven.

A large American flag was hoisted to the top of a telegraph pole. The band played patriotic music. Speeches were given. One railroad man said the promise of Christopher Columbus was now complete, "for this is the way to India."

The big moment finally arrived. The golden spike would be driven in by the top officers of the two companies, all of whom had been drinking champagne all morning. Leland Stanford, president of the Central Pacific Railroad Company and governor of California, rose to strike the first blow. He raised the sledge hammer over his head and brought it down. He missed and hit the rail. The Chinese workers of the Central Pacific smiled. Next came Thomas Durant of the Union Pacific Railroad Company. He, too, swung the sledge hammer. He missed and almost hit his foot. The Irish workers of the Union Pacific laughed—deep belly roars.

Lesser officials finally drove in the spike and excited telegraph operators clicked the news to the waiting country: THE GREAT PACIFIC RAILROAD IS COMPLETED.

In Chicago a parade of citizens formed and grew to be seven miles long. In Philadelphia the Liberty Bell chimed. In New York one hundred cannon fired salutes.

At Promontory Point, Utah, the two engines facing each other inched together until their pilots touched, and poet Bret Harte told what came next:

> This is what the engines said
> Unreported and unread...

Said the Engine from the West:
"I am from Sierra's crest;
And if altitude's a test,
Why, I reckon, its confessed
That I've done my level best."

Said the Engine from the East:
"They who work best talk the least.
S'pose you whistle down your brakes;
What you've done is no great shakes—
Pretty fair—but let our meeting
Be a different kind of greeting.
Let these folks with champagne stuffing
Not their Engines, do the puffing..."

It was over. East met West at Promontory Point, Utah. Twenty thousand men had hammered down 1,175 miles of track in just over three years. Scores of bridges had been erected and tunnels drilled. The Great Pacific Railroad had cost lives, blood, money, and muscle. Now, thank God, it was over.

That is what the Engines said
Unreported and unread
Spoken slightly through the nose
With a whistle at the close.

About the Author

R. Conrad Stein was born and grew up in Chicago. He enlisted in the Marine Corps at the age of eighteen, and served for three years. He then attended the University of Illinois, where he received a Bachelor's Degree in history. He later studied in Mexico and earned a Master of Fine Arts degree from the University of Guanajuato. He now lives in Mexico, where he is a member of the PEN writers group of San Miguel de Allende.

The study of history is Mr. Stein's hobby. Since he finds it to be an exciting subject, he tries to bring the excitement of history to his readers. He is the author of many other books, articles, and short stories written for young people.

About the Artist

Tom Dunnington divides his time between book illustration and wildlife painting. He has done many books for Childrens Press, as well as working on textbooks, and is a regular contributor to "Highlights for Children." He is at present working on his "Endangered Wildlife" series, which is being reproduced as limited edition prints. Tom lives in Elmhurst.